W9-CBC-390

J. Patrick Lewis

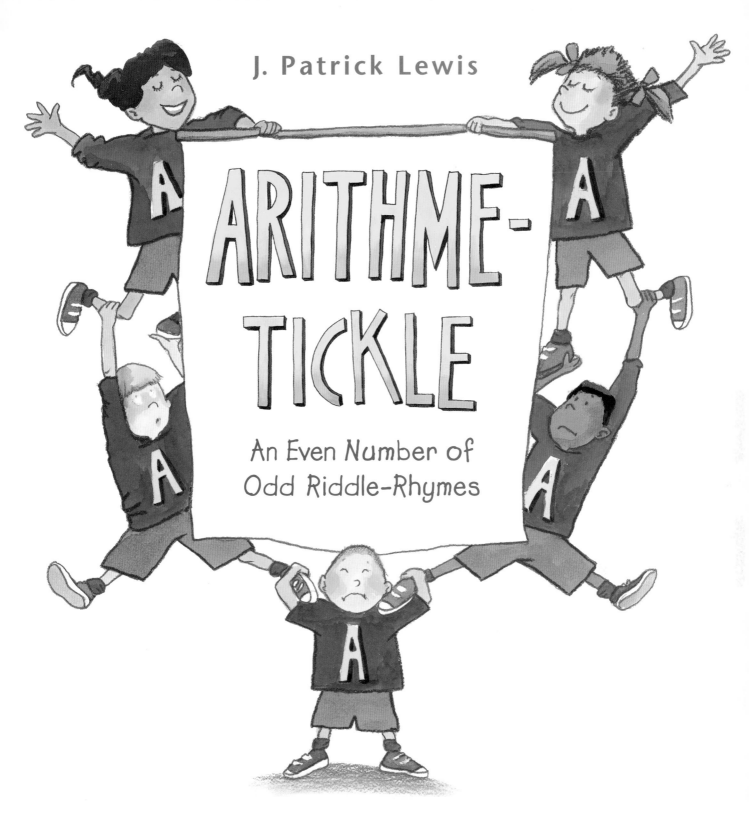

# ARITHME-TICKLE

### An Even Number of Odd Riddle-Rhymes

Illustrated by **Frank Remkiewicz**

*Silver Whistle*

Harcourt, Inc.  San Diego  New York  London

For Beth, Brian, and Cuba—
Again and always—J. P. L.

For Larry, Donna, Elaine, Sandi, and Dave
the arithme-ticklers at Paoli & Co.—F. R.

Text copyright © 2002 by J. Patrick Lewis
Illustrations copyright © 2002 by Frank Remkiewicz

Library of Congress Cataloging-in-Publication Data
Lewis, J. Patrick.
Arithme-tickle: an even number of odd riddle-rhymes/J. Patrick Lewis; illustrated by Frank Remkiewicz.
p. cm.
Summary: Rhyming text and illustrations present a variety of math problems.
1. Arithmetic—Juvenile literature. 2. Mathematical recreations—Juvenile literature. [1. Arithmetic.
2. Mathematical recreations.] I. Remkiewicz, Frank. II. Title.
QA115.L48 2002
513—dc21 2001003228
ISBN 0-15-216418-9

H G F E D C
Manufactured in China

The illustrations in this book were rendered in watercolor and Prisma colored pencils on Bristol Board.
The display type was created by Frank Remkiewicz.
The text type was set in Lemonade Bold.
Color separations by Bright Arts Ltd., Hong Kong
Manufactured by South China Printing Company, Ltd., China
This book was printed on totally chlorine-free Nymolla Matte Art paper.
Production supervision by Sandra Grebenar and Ginger Boyer
Designed by Frank Remkiewicz and Judythe Sieck

# CONTENTS

# The Mailman for the 92-Story Building

My ordinary day goes like this:
I start delivering mail on the 92nd floor,

Jog down 9 stories to the health spa,
Back up 4 floors to the plumbing company,
Ride the elevator down 25 flights
To the yo-yo office,

Fly up the stairs 2 floors
To Hot-Air Balloons Unlimited,
Drag myself up 6 more flights
To the Motorcycle Association,

Then drop into Bungee Cords, Inc.,
13 stories down.

Whew! I'm ready for lunch.
And the cafeteria's right here!
What floor am I on?

ANSWER: 92 − 9 + 4 − 25 + 2 + 6 − 13 = 57;
the cafeteria is on the 57th floor.

# A Regular Riddle

What's the number of points on a regular star,
Less the number of wheels on a regular car,
Plus the number of teeth in a regular mouth,
Less the number of states that begin with *South*,
Plus the number of paws on a malamute,
Plus the pairs of pants in a birthday suit,
Less the number of 17 brown bears' thumbs?
Easy, if you know your regular sums.

ANSWER: 5 − 4 + 32 − 2 + 4 + 0 − 34 = 1

# Going to Kalamazoo

It's 100 miles from me to you.
(You're in Detroit; I'm in Kalamazoo.)
How many miles do you think it would be
If we were halfway between you and me?

If you took a train to Kalamazoo
At 100 miles an hour (*choo-choo!*)
About what time would you get to me
If it left Detroit at half past three?

If you took the bus to Kalamazoo
At 50 miles an hour (*boo-hoo*),
And it made three 5-minute stops, then when
Would you get to me if you left at 10:00?

If you walked all the way to Kalamazoo —
And you walked 5 miles an hour (*moo-moo!*) —
Would you get there before the earth had spun
Around one time if you left at 1:00?

ANSWERS: 50 miles; 4:30; 12:15; yes, in 20 hours, walking time,
and it takes 24 hours for the earth to spin around.

# How to Hand-le a Horse

"It's a pleasure to measure a horse!"
Said the horse trainer Ernest P. Dithers.
"You must measure by hand and, of course,
You must go from the ground to the withers."

"If a pony stands 10 hands in all
From the ground to his shoulders (the withers),
And one hand is 4 inches, how tall
Is the pony?" said Ernest P. Dithers.

ANSWER: 4 + 4 + 4 + 4 + 4 + 4 + 4 + 4 + 4 + 4 = 40 inches
Or 10 hands times 4 inches per hand = 40 inches

10

# How to Weigh Your Poodle

Jennifer Hennessy
Took off her clothes
And stepped on the scale for fun.
The pointer, it started
To wiggle and jiggle
And settled on 71.

Then Jennifer Hennessy
Picked up her miniature
Poodle — here's Poo-poo-pee-doo.
Together they stood on the scale
And weighed a grand total of 92.

Well, Poo-poo-pee-doo
Is a bit overgrown.
How much does
Poo-poo-pee-doo
Weigh alone?

ANSWER: 92 pounds – 71 pounds = 21 pounds

11

# Sailing a Bathtub

Columbus sailed the ocean (blue)
In what year? I don't know. Do you?

Francesca sailed a bathtub (white)
In 1412 one Saturday night.

How many years before his trip
Did little Francesca take her dip?

ANSWER: If Columbus sailed in 1492, then Francesca got
her bath 80 years before Columbus came to America
(1492 – 1412 = 80).

# Jumping on the Moon

Neil Armstrong could jump three feet in the air
In Wapakoneta, Ohio.

But then he became the first astronaut
To land on the moon, and my, oh

My, you can jump six times as high on the moon
As in Wapakoneta.

How high could he jump on the moon (which is *not*
Green cheese or Swiss or feta)?

ANSWER: 3 + 3 + 3 + 3 + 3 + 3 = 18
Or 3 feet times 6 = 18 feet.
So Neil Armstrong could jump 18 feet on
the moon—if he had really wanted to!

# Finger Play

Hold up your fingers (and your thumbs).
Here's a trick I do
If I want to multiply by 9.
You try it, too.

Take 2 times 9.
Fold down your second finger
from the left (when you times 2).
Understand? Just read your hand —
It's the easiest thing to do.
1 finger, then a blank between
the other 8, which makes 18.

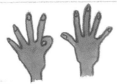 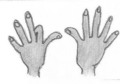

Now try again.
5 times 9, 8 times 9, 4 times 9...,

Soon they'll be calling you Einstein.

# The Polka-Dot Pajama Bird

In 50 days the polka-dot
Pajama bird had flown
From a polka-dotted birdhouse
To the park at Yellowstone.
She didn't stop at birdbaths,
Puddles, pools, or water fountains
Until she reached the Pink Pajama
Polka-dotted mountains.

The flight? 5,000 miles or so.
How far did Miss Pajama go
On average each of 50 days
To bag pink polka-dotted rays?

ANSWER: She flew 5,000 miles
in 50 days, or 100 miles per day.

# Arithme-Riddles

Dr. Nast said, "I'll give you three shots
to get rid of those hideous spots.
One shot every half hour." Goodness' sake!
How long did those nasty Nast shots take?

ANSWER: Shot #1 + 1/2 hour,
Shot #2 + 1/2 hour,
Shot #3 and finished!
Or 1 hour to take all 3 shots.

Farmer Flynn had 20 sheep.
All but 9 sheep died.
Now you decide:
How many sheep does Flynn still keep?

ANSWER: 9

A hole is 3 feet long, 4 feet wide,
And 5 feet deep, you dig?
How much dirt can be removed
From a hole that big?

Answer: None. A hole doesn't
have any dirt in it.

20

# How Many Coconuts?

How many palm trees swaying in the breeze?
How many hives for the bumblebees?
How many warthogs in a quartet?
How many apes eating apes suzette?
How many rings on the ring-tailed cat?
How many parakeets having a chat?
How many snakes are taking a snooze?
How many toads with wart tattoos?
How many toes on the three-toed sloth?
How many bats are chasing one moth?
How many coconuts earthward bound?
How many coconuts lying on the ground?
How many monkeys sitting in a tree?
How many coconuts fell on me?

(Add up all How manys, then
Check your answer once again.)

ANSWER: 6 + 3 + 4 + 1 + 5 + 7 + 2 + 4 + 12 + 2 + 4 + 10 + 3 + 1 = 64

# Gas: $1.00 a Gallon

My dad filled up the Chevy
For about a buck per gallon,
And drove us to New York—me
And my buddies Benny and Alan.

"I'd pay for gas," he said, "but if
We split it—each one quarter—
I'll buy you boys a dinner
At the Pennsylvania border."

How much did each one owe him if
The tank held twenty gallons?
(In other words, my share's the same
As Benny's, Dad's, and Alan's.)

Oh, Benny, Al, and I ate foot-long
Hot dogs till we burst,
But Dad made sure that I
And my two buddies paid him first!

ANSWER: $20.00 = $5.00 + $5.00 + $5.00 + $5.00
Or $5.00 each

# Early One Morning

The rooster crowed at 6:03,
The pig got up at 8:15.
What time did Farmer Ben awake
If he woke up halfway between
The time the rooster and the pig
Got out of bed? Oops . . . I forgot!
Ben waited 15 minutes more —
Until he smelled the coffeepot.

ANSWER: If Farmer Ben got up halfway between the time the rooster and the pig awoke, that would have been 7:09 A.M. Since he waited 15 minutes longer, he actually got up at 7:24 A.M.

# Your Average Cow

Your average cow lives to age 15 —
Some live longer now and then.
The average human? 75.
(Women live longer than men.)

So we live to be how many times
As old as your average cow?
If you guess the answer correctly,
Go ahead and take a bow.

ANSWER: 15 + 15 + 15 + 15 + 15 = 75
Or 15 times 5 = 75, so 5 times as old.

# Thomasina's Eggs

It's been about 4 weeks,
And now I hear 2 squeaks,
And now I see 2 beaks
Of turkey chicks appearing.

How many eggs have hatched?
How many chick-chicks scratched?
How many holes unpatched?
With Thomasina cheering?

ANSWER: 4 eggs – 2 eggs = 2 eggs

# The Tortoise and the Hare

Thomas Tortoise crawls 1 mile a day.
Jane Hare can run 1 mile an hour.

How much faster is Jane Hare if
She's using all her jet hare-power?*

*That's not the actual gap perhaps,
If Jane insists on taking naps.

ANSWER: Thomas Tortoise crawls
1 mile a day. Jane Hare runs
1 mile an hour. Since
1 day = 24 hours, Jane Hare can
run 1 times 24 = 24 times faster than
Thomas Tortoise . . . without
the naps.

# Pardon My Yardstick

A yardstick is how many inches long?
Take half of that.
Subtract the number of lives
Of any given cat.
Now add the number of eggs
In a normal egg carton.
Subtract the average age
Of a kid in kindergarten.
Add the syllable at the end of
TIMBUK_____.

I ended up with half a yardstick.
How about you?

TIMBUK

## The Cat and Dog Letters

Dear Ms. Cat,

I of-10 go to T at 3.
I 1-der, would U dine with me?
And if U 1 2 roller sk-8,
Please come at 2—don't hesit-8!

Yours drooly,

Marv L. S. Dog

Dear Mr. Dog,

A K-9 T at 3? Why, yes!

At sk-8-ing I'm a gr-8 6-cess!

And I'll wear something just 4 U —

A pina-4 and a 2-2, 2!

Fur Ever,

B. U. Tiffle Cat

# Plus and Minus

If you are most particular,
Curved, straight, or perpendicular
(That is, arithme-ticular!)
And don't confuse a minus with a plus,

Then no amount can trounce you
Because by all accounts you
Are ready! I pronounce you
Mr. or Ms. Arithme-ticulous!